To

From

To Mum and Dad, with love J.S.

Text by Christina Goodings
Illustrations copyright © 2013 Janet Samuel
This edition copyright © 2013 Lion Hudson

The right of Janet Samuel to be identified as the illustrator of this work has been asserted by her in accordance with the Copyright, Designs and Patents Act 1988.

Published by Lion Children's Books
an imprint of
Lion Hudson plc
Wilkinson House, Jordan Hill Road,
Oxford OX2 8DR, England
www.lionhudson.com/lionchildrens

ISBN 978 0 7459 6350 1

First edition 2013

Acknowledgments
Bible extracts are taken or adapted from the Good News Bible published by the Bible Societies and HarperCollins Publishers, © American Bible Society 1994, used with permission.

The Lord's Prayer (on page 37) as it appears in *Common Worship: Services and Prayers for the Church of England* (Church House Publishing, 2000) is copyright © The English Language Liturgical Consultation and is reproduced by permission of the publisher.

Prayers by Christina Goodings, Lois Rock, and Sophie Piper are copyright © Lion Hudson.
All prayers are by Christina Goodings except:
p.9 Sarah Betts Rhodes (1829–1904)
p.13 Sophie Piper
pp.17, 21, 33, 41, 57 Lois Rock

A catalogue record for this book is available
from the British Library

Printed and bound in China, March 2013, LH23

BIBLE
AND PRAYERS

for Teddy and Me

Retold by Christina Goodings
Illustrated by Janet Samuel

LION
CHILDREN'S

Contents

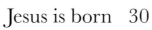

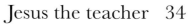

In the beginning

In the beginning, there was nothing.
Then God spoke: "Let there be light!"

God made the world and everything in it:
God put birds in the sky, fish in the sea,
and plants that grow tall in the golden sunshine.
God made all the animals and God made
people to take care of the wonderful world.

God also made the night:
the dark sky, the silver moon, the twinkly stars.
And when you and I are fast asleep, God is
watching over all the world.

ZZZZZZ

God, who made the earth,
The air, the sky, the sea,
Who gave the light its birth,
Careth for me.

God, who made the grass,
The flower, the fruit, the tree,
The day and night to pass,
Careth for me.

God, who made all things,
On earth, in air, in sea,
Who changing seasons brings,
Careth for me.

Noah and the ark

The raindrops spattered on the roof of the ark.

pitter   patter

The raindrops fell into the great big flood.
"God sent the rain to wash away the bad old
world," said Noah to his family.
"But we are safe on the ark: you and me and two
of every kind of animal."

splish splash

After many days and many weeks, the flood ended.
God put a rainbow in the sky.

"It's a sign of my promise," said God. "I will never
again send a flood like that.

"There will be summer and winter, a time to sow
seeds and a time to harvest crops for ever."

Rainbow reaching up so high:
may the sun shine in the sky.

Rainbow reaching to the ground:
may the rain fall all around.

As the seasons come and go,
may God bless this earth below.

May the springtime seeds unfold;
may the harvest ripen gold.

Baby Moses

From her hiding place among the reeds, Miriam heard soldiers marching.

The king had told his soldiers to kill baby boys. She made herself very small. They mustn't see her.

Most of all, they mustn't see her baby brother in his floating cradle.

They marched on by.

"God must be looking after us," thought Miriam.

15

Now some women were coming to the river to bathe.
  One of them was the princess of Egypt.
  She saw the cradle.
  She saw the baby.
  "I love him," she said. "I am going to call him
Moses, and I'm going to keep him safe."
  Miriam knew for sure. God was looking after
everything.

God, look down from heaven:
Here on earth you'll see
Someone looking upwards –
That someone is me.

David and Goliath

Goliath was mocking the soldiers. "Does anyone dare fight me?

"If any of you cowards can beat me, you win the war."

"But he's so tall," whispered the soldiers.

"Look at his armour!"

"Look at his sharp weapons glinting in the sunshine."

"I dare," said David. "I trust in God."

GRRRR

19

poinng

David the shepherd boy put a stone
in his sling and threw.
   Goliath fell down.
   God had helped David win.

Sometimes troubles seem so big
and I feel very small.
But God is love, and God is strength:
I need not fear at all.

Jonah learns a lesson

If Jonah hadn't been running from God, he wouldn't have been on the boat.

If he hadn't been on the boat, there wouldn't have been a storm.

If there hadn't been a storm, he wouldn't have been thrown into the sea.

But now he was sinking down, down, down.

Aargh

God sent a huge sea creature. It swallowed Jonah and swam him to shore.

"I'm sorry," said Jonah to God. "I shall do what you asked."

He went to Nineveh. He told the people there to
mend their wicked ways.

The people said sorry to God.

And God forgave them.

"I knew you'd do that," said Jonah. "You forgive
everyone, however bad they've been."

24

I cannot ever run from God
I cannot ever hide
Not even if I try to sail
Across the ocean wide.

I need not ever run from God
I need not try to hide
For God wants me to be his friend
His arms are open wide.

Daniel and the lions

Three men went to the king and bowed low.

"O King," they said. "Someone is breaking the law."

"Who?" asked the king. "What law?"

"Your new law," they replied, "about not saying prayers.

Your Majesty

26

"Daniel is still saying prayers to his God."

"That's no problem," said the king. "He's still my best helper."

"It's a big problem," said the men. "Your law says Daniel must be thrown to the lions."

purrr

Daniel was thrown to the lions.
  The king worried about him all night.
  But God sent an angel to keep Daniel safe.
  Next morning, the king found him alive and well.
"Bring Daniel back out," he said. "I want everyone to
know that Daniel's God is great and good."

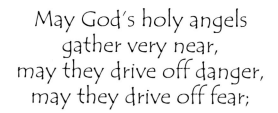

May God's holy angels
gather very near,
may they drive off danger,
may they drive off fear;

may they guide my doing,
may they help my prayer,
may I feel God's angels
with me everywhere.

Jesus is born

Joseph held the door wide and shepherds trooped into the stable.

"There's the baby in the manger!" they said.

Mary smiled as she listened to their story.

"Out on the hillside, an angel came and told us about the baby," they said. "He has been sent by God to bless the world."

31

The wise men brought out gold, frankincense, and myrrh.

"We saw a new star," they said. "It is the sign that a new king has been born.

"It led the way here to Bethlehem."

They gave their gifts to Mary's baby, Jesus: God's newborn king.

The stars that shine at Christmas
Shine on throughout the year;
Jesus, born so long ago,
Still gathers with us here.

We listen to his stories,
We learn to say his prayer,
We follow in his footsteps
And learn to love and share.

33

Jesus the teacher

Jesus grew up. He knew that God had work for him to do. He became a teacher, telling people how to be God's friends.

"Never try to get your own back," he told them.

"Show love and kindness to everyone, even those who are unkind to you.

"Look at the way God feeds the birds and clothes the flowers. Trust that God will look after you.

"When you pray, go into your room and close the door.

"You don't need lots of clever words. God already knows what you need.

"Here is a prayer for always:"

Our Father in heaven,
hallowed be your name,
your kingdom come,
your will be done,
on earth as in heaven.
Give us today our daily bread.
Forgive us our sins
as we forgive those who sin against us.
Lead us not into temptation
but deliver us from evil.

The story of the sower

Jesus told this story.

"A man went out to sow seeds in his field.

"Some fell on the path. Birds came and ate them.

"Some fell on rocky ground. The roots had nowhere to grow, and the seedlings wilted in the sun.

"Some fell among weeds. The seedlings were choked by the stronger plants.

"Some fell on good soil and grew to give a good harvest.

peck

peck
peck

"The story has a meaning," said Jesus.

"My teaching is like scattered seed.

"Some people are like seeds on the path. They hear my words and then forget them.

"Some are like seeds on rocky ground. They start to follow my teaching but give up when it gets hard.

"Some are like seeds among weeds. They let all kinds of things get in the way of obeying what I say.

"Some are like seeds on good soil.
  "They hear my teaching.
  "They learn to obey it.
  "They produce a harvest of good deeds."

I'm learning to be more like Jesus,
I'm learning the right way to live.
I'm learning to show loving kindness,
I'm learning to truly forgive.

The lost sheep

Jesus also told this story.

  "There was once a shepherd who had a hundred sheep.

  "One day, when he was counting them, he found that there were only 99.

  "He left them safely nibbling green grass.

  "He went to find his lost sheep.

Bye

43

baa

"When he found it, he was overjoyed.

"Gently he carried it home.

"He called to his friends. 'Let's have a party!
I have found my lost sheep.'

"God is like that shepherd," said Jesus. "God
is seeking for all those who have wandered away
from the right path.

"When they are found, all the angels sing."

Dear Father God and Shepherd:
sometimes,
especially after mischief,
I am afraid that no one loves me –
not even me.

Please come and find me.
Please bring me gently home.
Let me hear the angels sing.

The farmer's son

The young man emptied the bucket of swill.
The pigs came squealing and gobbled it up.

"They have food," he sighed. "I'm starving.

"I wasted all the money my father let me have.

"Now I have to do this horrid job for almost no pay."

Then he had an idea.

"I shall go home to my father. I shall say I am sorry. I shall ask for a job on the family farm."

oink

46

oink

47

He walked the long miles home.
  From far away his father saw him.
  He came running to hug him.
  "I'm very sorry about everything I wasted,"
said the young man.
  "All I care about," replied his father, "is that you're
home again.
  "Now it's time for a party!"

Dear God,
Thank you for love.
Thank you for forgiveness.
Thank you for blowing away the
clouds of sadness
and giving us joy and sunshine.

The man in the tree

The people of Jericho didn't like Zacchaeus.

"He makes us pay too much tax money," they complained. "He's a nasty cheat!"

So when Zacchaeus joined the crowd who wanted to see Jesus, everyone elbowed him to the back.

Oh

Zacchaeus climbed a tree.
Then Jesus came and stopped underneath it.
"Come down, Zacchaeus," he called out. "I want to
stay at your house."

Zacchaeus gave Jesus a feast. He listened to what Jesus had to say. It made him think.

Then he stood up. "I'm sorry about cheating," he said. "I'm going to mend my ways and repay everyone."

"Good," said Jesus. "I came to help people turn their lives around."

jingle jingle

If I find myself
on the downhill road
to doing things
that are wrong,
I will turn around
and ask God to help
bring me back to where I belong.

The good Samaritan

Just how do you do what God wants?
  Jesus told this story to explain.
  "There was once a man who went on a journey.
Robbers came and beat him up and left him in the
road.

Eek

"A priest from the Temple came along. He saw the man and hurried past.

"A helper at the Temple came along. He came and looked at the man. Then he hurried away.

Dear me

clip clop

"A Samaritan came along. He had nothing to do with the Temple. People looked down on him for that.

"Yet when he saw the man, he hurried to help him.

"Which of the three people did as God wants?" asked Jesus.

The answer was easy: the one who was kind.

Dear God,
When I see someone in trouble,
may I know when to stop and help
and when to hurry to fetch help;
but may I never pass by,
pretending I did not see.

The first Easter

All kinds of people thought Jesus was great.

"He shows us the way to be part of God's loving family," they agreed.

Other people did not like Jesus.

"We will have him put to death on a cross," they said.

Jesus' friends were sad.

In spite of the hurt, Jesus knew he must love his enemies. "Father God, forgive them," he prayed.

Jesus died and was buried. Three days later, his friends saw him. By a miracle, he was alive again. Then they knew for sure: God's love is stronger than anything.

Master

After Jesus went to heaven, his friends remembered what he had said:

"Don't be worried. I am going to my Father's house. I will make ready a place for you.

"Here on earth, God's spirit will help you do what is good and right."

The autumn leaves were laid to rest
But now the trees are green,
And signs that God brings all to life
Throughout the world are seen.

And Jesus is alive, they say,
And death is not the end.
We rise again in heaven's light
With Jesus as our friend.

Dear God,
Please be my special friend;
closer than a hug,
softer than a quilt,
braver – far braver –
than even my best-loved bear and me
together.